Beneath the Clay

ISBN: 1-4392-0980-4

ISBN-13: 9781439209806

Visit www.booksurge.com to order additional copies.

Beneath the Clay

Tyler K. Hill

I N MAY 1982 I visited Glengariff for the first time, finding lodging at the Blue Pool Hotel, a stately well-furnished building with an extensive collection of art and antiques. The hotel had its own bar with plush furniture. While I was having a pint during my first day there, an English couple approximately my age introduced themselves to me. The gentleman had been to Ireland before but it was the first time for the lady to visit the country. Their trip was in celebration of her birthday, his gift to her. The following is an account of the camaraderie that grew from that first meeting.

Glengariff

I HAVE SPENT MANY moments today in laughter over last night's conversation with the Blue Pool Hotel's bartender, John Connelly. He appears to be in his late sixties or early seventies, with the gift of conversation frequently associated with the Irish in legend and fact and can sway from humor to sternness fluidly in an instant without altering character. Christine, Richard, John and I sat up until after 3 a.m. last night drinking, talking, and eventually arguing. All was friendly.

Christine, Richard and I spent yesterday afternoon exploring the magnificent, wild countryside in Glengariff. We walked to the mountains around 12:30 p.m., and visited the noted walks. Small wooden arrow-shaped signs alerted us to points of interest. One such spot is "Lady Bantree's Lookout." Off the winding road is an upward path that is guided by a stony wall. The trees and rocks are more often than not moss-covered, and shamrocks abound nearly everywhere. On the way up to the lookout, Christine noted, "I'll bet the leprechauns live around here." "Oh, sure they do," I agreed. It became a topic of the walk and soon we named the area beneath "Lady Bantree's Lookout" Leprechaun Forest. We began pointing to hollow sections of tree trunks. "Now there's a leprechaun's house." Or spotting a stream with a piece of bark floating in it, "Well, look, there's a leprechaun's canoe." A stretch of vine became a clothesline, a leaf a bath towel. A chestnut shell was a cauldron and an acorn a drinking goblet.

We came across an abandoned rusted green bicycle. "It must have been left by a leprechaun," I said, after examining it and finding the chain broken. "No, can't you see it's too big for a leprechaun?" Christine corrected. "Oh, yes, you're right. How silly of me."

The three of us had dinner together in the elegantly furnished dining room here at the Blue Pool Hotel. Richard and I had grilled whiting, Christine had sole. We shared a bottle of French white wine. After dinner, it was back to the sitting-drinking parlor. We began telling John of the very exciting walks we had during the day. The day had been divided into two journeys. The first was our walk, which covered around six miles. The second journey was by car to Barley Lake. Richard drove us as far as the road went, then we were to walk the rest of the way to the lake. Howling winds and swift, sudden rains are no detractions for a spring day in Ireland. Atop Barley Lake the winds wildly rippled the water, the clouds swept over the crags and the darkness of mid-afternoon heightened the tone of the yellow gorse. Within this view, for miles, there were no other people. It was landscape material for a painting by John Martin. When we told John about going to "Lady Bantree's Lookout" I interjected, "I never believed in them until today. But I must tell you that I found proof on this day of something I've always heard of - The Leprechauns."

"What!!?" John asked.

"Yes! Now I know about what the Irish always speak of. We found leprechaun houses and all sorts of evidence of the little people."

"Oh, come on now," he said suspiciously. "Do you mean to tell me that you really believe what you're saying?"

I thought that because of the total absurdity of my statements, he would know that I was only amusing myself. But he felt I'd been convinced of the existence of the little people and his growing exasperation unintentionally spurred me on to be all the more ridiculous.

Christine picked up on cue, as if a script had been written. "John, we saw their little houses today," referring to the moss-encrusted openings beneath the tree roots we had seen. "I must say I hadn't taken them for real either but today I found out for myself."

John showed his disbelief and gave a careful grin. "Oh, come on. How can you be so gullible?"

"But, John," Christine and I said in unison, "we saw their homes. I found little pairs of green shoes and tiny clothes lines of a leprechaun's laundry today."

"Oh, come on. Do you really expect me to believe this!?"

"We know it sounds a bit off, but we saw these things," Christine told him.

"How can you be so gullible?" he said again.

"You know, John," I said, "Richard is the most reserved of the three of us and he found it hard to accept at first." Turning to Richard, I said, "Tell him -didn't you become convinced of the leprechauns today?"

Richard nodded and said, "I must say it was the most peculiar sight I've ever seen. Here were these tiny bits of clothing hanging out to dry near those tree-trunk houses."

John began to lose his patience. "What do you take me for, a lunatic!" "No, John, we are not lunatics either but we did see these things."

"Oh, my goodness. This is just awful. All this talk about leprechauns as if they exist."

Richard played his pan well, as the levelheaded one who held out his disbelief until all the evidence was in. He assured John, "I can only tell you that I scorned Christine and Tyler until I saw those clothes lines myself."

"Come on now. You are making a mockery of Ireland now."

In front of me on the small coffee table set a triangular-shaped ashtray. In it were molded three circles of about an inch in diameter. I picked up the ashtray and said, "See these circles - you may call me a lunatic but today we also found a tiny bicycle with wheels about the size of these circles. It had to belong to a leprechaun. What else?"

"Oh, my God! You are completely mad, my man. How can you say such things?"

"John, I wish I had the cycle with me but I didn't have the heart to take it from which ever fellow or lass owned it."

"Oh, my God, for Christ's sake! You are all mad!"

Christine came in, "But, John, you know us. We are not mad. We are just telling you what we saw. It was hard for us to accept at first, but it was simply that we saw these things."

"Oh, my God. This is a disgrace! I've been in the tourism business for forty years and never have I heard such nonsense! All this damn foolish talk of leprechauns and such!"

"But, John,...."

"But, John, nothing. I'm a peaceful man and I can only give you sound advice. Don't go saying a word of this to anyone else in Ireland. It's trouble you'll be getting yourself into if you go on about this lunacy."

Respecting the gentleman, I did not remind him that half the economy of Killarney is guided by such lunacy.

John's consternation with Christine, Richard and me abated and the following night we were all back in the bar of the Blue Pool Hotel until closing time. Glengariff has a few, as opposed to several pubs, and with John being a draw for many of the locals, the hotel was visited by quite a few friends during the course of that night's criss-crossing of drink. Although we had not met any of the gents who came in for a few rounds before moving on, Christine, Richard and I were invited to go along

with the various crews as they re-entered the night. Christine and Richard would be leaving on the drive to Dublin the next morning before returning to England. We were content to stay at the hotel with John, since that night would pass soon enough without additional ramblings. John closed down the bar around 1 am allowing me an order of a pint and a double whiskey to take up to my room, where, after bidding goodnight and farewell to my new English friends, I sat in the quiet of my room before tossing a shoe several times at a spider crawling on the ceiling. It survived the attacks so I turned out the lights and hoped for the best.

The next morning there was a knocking on my door. A moment of neglect had given me another opportunity to have a parting word with Christine. "We'll be off now, but I thought I'd just come up and say good-bye with this," as she handed me my cap. "You left it in the bar last night in your drunken stupor and you just wouldn't be the same without this thing that you wear on your head."

It was nearly ten o'clock and it was soon before the end of breakfast service so I thanked Christine as she left, then got myself as presentable as possible to go downstairs to the dining room. I was the last resident of the day to have breakfast and I was happy to have the room to myself, sharing the morning with a pot of tea. I am much better off not talking to strangers after a night's drinking.

My first pint of the day came at the hotel around two o'clock after a long walk around the wooded sanctuaries of Glengariff. Three young locals came in for a Saturday afternoon of drink and relaxation. In a word they were scruffs. Two were quiet and one was quietly brash. Another fellow came into the room and ordered a pint and a measure of Paddy's. Charming in his state of drunkenness, he told silly jokes.

"Why do ducks have webbed feet?"

"To stomp out forest fires."

"Why do elephants have large feet?"

"To stomp out burning ducks."

"Har, har, har! I know I'm half pissed, but I'll finish the job right here and be totally pissed before the day is done. Har, har, har! What a lovely way to be on a Saturday afternoon."

Everyone in the room was grist for his mill of self-entertainment. He obviously had a history of holding court and was well known by everyone, from John to the other customers, to the groundskeepers, to the chambermaid, who sat smoking Silk Cut cigarettes, see-sawing her crossed legs, saying nothing but smiling at his humor. By way of introduction to me he said, "What are you doing here?"

"I'm on vacation, or on holiday as you would say." I replied. "How do you like it here?" "I like it here very much."

"Hmm. Good."

His comrades didn't say a thing; just sat there sipping their pints, enjoying the room on a Saturday afternoon. They had contented lethargy, not drunk yet, although one of the silent fellows soon had his chin on his chest, dozing off with a half pint on the table before him. But they had been drunk the night before, had not gotten much sleep, and then had gotten an early afternoon's start on pints to relieve their hangovers, just to take the edge off. More silly jokes resumed from the spokesman and soon Paddy Downing, the owner of the hotel, came in to, as a jazz musician would say, sit in on a session. He was a large and friendly gentleman.

"Well, here he is himself, the man who owns half the village," the half-pissed spokesman announced, laughing to himself. I was about to leave the room for a walk in the village when Paddy ordered a round of drinks on the house, which John cheerily produced. One of the drunks was still asleep so he was shaken from his rest and told it was time to wake up and drink some more.

"Quite right, quite right." A lift of the glass to his lips, a trail of stout down his shirt and " Ahhhhh!"

I went to the Blue Loo pub that night. A group of fiddle, guitar, accordion and bodhran provided music.

The pub was crowded and I was not able to get a seat at the bar, but shared a table with happy strangers. Time went very quickly enjoying the atmosphere with the strangers and returning to the bar to make my way through the loud crowd for a few rounds of pints. Paddy Downing and a couple of his attendants entered and his seniority in the village had an occupied table automatically vacated for him. He called from his table and invited me. Mr. Downing, his company and I shared rounds until the music and boisterousness flowed into closing time. At that time I was informed that I would be expected at Sunday mass at the village church in the morning.

I had enough sense to ask when the last service would be. Relieved to hear that the last mass would begin at eleven, I parted company with my hosts, walked the short distance to the hotel and fell asleep shortly after reaching my bed.

I had just enough time for breakfast the following morning before leaving the hotel for mass. The church's steeple bell was pealing as I joined the village congregation on its walk to mass. I was one of many who had chosen to visit the last hour of salvation. It was my first time at a Catholic mass and enjoyed the rituals, watching but not walking to receive Holy Communion.

When the service ended, I was walking down the steps of the church and a voice greeted, "Hello, How are you today?" I turned and saw Paddy walking with a lady I thought I recognized but could not be sure.

I was aware that a legendary Irish actress still called Ireland home and it was

Glengariff that she had chosen while not making films in America. "Have you met our friend from America?" Paddy asked the lady. "No, but I have seen you in the village," she said to me. "Well, that being the case, I'd like to properly introduce you two," Paddy added. I expressed my pleasure of making her acquaintance. It was not a proper moment for me to mention my decades long admiration for her work. She extended her hand, saying, "It is nice to meet you. I'm sure I'll be seeing more of you in the village." I thanked her, thanked Paddy, wished them both a good Sunday afternoon, walked to the news agent for the Sunday papers and read the news in the courtyard of the hotel until the bar opened at the hotel at three o'clock.

The Boot

WHILE OUT ON the mountains by Barley Lake a gust of wind threw me from one of the rocks and in my fall the heel of my left boot fell off. I spent the next two hours with one leg shorter than the other. Afterwards, I walked through the village carrying the heel-less boot. Christine recommended that I take the boot to an elderly couple, who live in their version of a non-edible gingerbread house and general store. The front room before their private living quarters has all sorts of little rubber bugs, toys, candy dispensers, leather watch bands with rusted buckles, cardboard comb holders with warped edges and faded print, dust covered souvenir ashtrays, decades old travel brochures and various other bits of junk. A portion of the shop was also equipped for shoe repair. I took the boot to the shop, introduced myself to the woman of the house and asked her if her husband could fix it for me.

"Well, let's see now. I don't know when he'll be here," she said. "Myself, I should be out in the morning, and he should be in around noon. Then again, he may show up tonight and I may not be away in the morning."

I handed her the boot and severed heel saying, "Thank you. I'll stop here tomorrow at two in the afternoon. Someone is sure to be here then."

"Oh, yes. Quite right. Yes, indeed. We'll get your boot all fixed and ready for you by then. Yes, indeed. Two o'clock it is."

I returned to their shop at two o'clock the following day. The woman was sitting behind the counter knitting a young child's sweater. Behind her on a shelf sat the boot and heel, still separated. They hadn't been moved since I'd last seen them the previous day. A very cheerful "Well, hello" from the woman.

"I'm afraid we don't have your boot ready just yet. I showed it to my husband this morning and he intended to get to it but after tea went across the street to the pub."

I told her, "That's all right for now but I'll be leaving tomorrow and must have it fixed by morning."

"Oh, yes, yes, he'll get on with it and I'll drop it off for you before you leave."

The next morning after breakfast at the hotel I returned to their home and passing through the front door, I noticed out of the corner of my right eye a figure behind the counter. There was a palsied, unshaven man, his crouched figure shadowing in uncertainty over my boot.

"Good morning to you. I see you are working on my boot."

"Hmmm?" he uttered, looking blindly at the heel in his hands, the rest of the boot sitting on his lap. "Yes. I don't think much can be done for this." He held the heel up towards me. "I put a nail in the bottom here. I'm trying to figure out a way to pound it into the rest of the boot and then bend it over inside so you don't have to walk on it."

His eyes were equivalent to that of a sea bass looking up from a dinner plate. His face was a road map of broken capillaries. His voice that of a mouth permanently fixed with an unswallowable wad of porridge.

The wife entered the room to see how the job was coming along.

"Don't worry," I told her. "I'll take the boot with me and will find someone, maybe in Cork, who will fix it." I didn't tell her that I'd found another man in the village who could do the job for me. Her husband then extended both boot and heel towards me with the added characteristic contribution of a large drop of his spittle running down the side of each.

On that note I said my good-bye. I took the boot to the home of a gentleman I had rented a bicycle from days earlier for riding around Bantree Bay. Stricken with polio during childhood, he had learned early how to spend time alone productively at home. In adulthood he spent his time renting bicycles and repairing shoes. He lived and worked in a cottage connected to a row of one story buildings. The home had old, faded wallpaper and his floors were naked, scarred wood. He lived alone, and on his living room walls hung newspaper clippings of weddings in his family, poignant reminders of the wedding he never had. They were happy memories of his family rather than morbid indications of loneliness.

I asked him if he could have the boot repaired by one o'clock and he smiled back. "Good man! I'll have it for you then." At one o'clock I returned to his home and saw him through the window. I waved and he did the same. My boot was intact and waiting for me. Before I left we had a talk of what is best called this and that, with the expressed hope of meeting again.

He seemed content in his life. He had that aloneness which should not be mistaken for loneliness. Loneliness is very well hidden by the busy.

The Pensioner

WHILE VISITING KILLARNEY I stayed at Courtney's, a rough working class bar until closing time one night, sitting at a table next to an elderly couple exchanging questions about their occupations. The gentleman was neatly dressed in a well-worn blue suit. The lady had prepared for her evening of craique by applying a quarter-inch pancake makeup to her cheeks. The two shared pints, questions and tales.

"What line of work are you in?" the gentleman asked.

"I'm a school teacher," the lady said.

"A teacher! Indeed, indeed. Myself, I was almost made a school master myself."

"When was this?"

"In 1922."

"Well, what do you do now?"

"I'm on pension."

"From what?"

"From farming."

"What? Not from teaching?"

"No, after I wasn't made school master, I went back to farming."

"Where is your farm?"

"Well, it's like this you see. I became poor in health and had to sell the farms."

"Farms? How many did you have?"

"Well, you see, I had two farms and because of my health I sold 'em."

"What's wrong with your health?"

"Well, y'see, I'm a diabetic."

"And it's drinkin' you're doin'. Isn't that bad for your condition?"

"Well, it's like this now. My doctor told me not to mix my tablets with my drink. So today I'm off the tablets and on the drink."

"That's right stupid, isn't it?"

"No, my doctor told me that if I only have two pints a day when I'm off the tablets I'm all right. And this is only my second pint today."

They remained there drinking, enjoying one another's company. I finished my pint and left the crowded bar wishing them well in any and all yarns they would spin in the future.

Halloween

I SIT AT A table in the lounge bar of Ashford House in Arklow, having just eaten my dinner of pork chops and chips in an adjoining room.

There is a band of two for the entertainment of the customers. A guitar player and a singer, who imitates Elvis Presley, as they play American country music.

I have only seen a few children dressed up for Halloween. One girl of around eight years old came into the bar where I sat before having dinner. She was not elaborately dressed, but carried a tattered woolen bag and opened it with a shy look in her eyes. Some of the customers sitting at the bar ignored her as though it were a daily ritual, but when she came to me, I placed in a ten pence coin.

To my left sat an old woman, who spoke to me through scattered, darkened teeth and told me that today was her sixty-eighth birthday. Since this pub was dimly lit and because a few adults had come in wearing Halloween masks, the woman took me by surprise. I was sitting with my pint of Guinness, relaxing after a very tiring twelve-mile walk from Glendelough. I spotted a hunched figure carrying an empty glass and a bottle of Guinness. I noticed what appeared to be a fright wig accompanied by a matching facemask of The Old Hag. The entire visage was creased with deep overlapping lines. All elasticity gone from the face, indentations around the mouth where the lips fell into the shallow section where teeth once were. The chin protruded with a mole and a single hair pointing skyward.

The figure came for a seat and I noticed that there was no make-up or mask. The old woman sat down and swayed to the music of Elvis. She sat there, smoking, drinking and raising her glass to the singer. After each song she clapped and said, "Good man! Thank you very much!" as if each song were played in honor of her birthday. She got up to "dance" for each of Elvis' songs. She wobbled on her feet each time getting up from her seat and nearly fell over a few times. She was unsuccessful at several attempts to solicit a dancing partner. Not even Elvis was interested.

She returned after one of her rug-cuttings and muttered to me, "It's my birthday and I've got two sons. But do you think either one of them would help me celebrate my birthday? No! My husband died two years ago and there is no one to look after an old woman." Fearing she was about to ask me for the next dance, I rose from my chair, went over to the bar and bought a bottle of Guinness for the old woman.

Returning, I presented her with the drink and said, "Happy Birthday." I held back from saying, "Happy Halloween." She simply looked and acted too much a representation of the holiday to be reminded of it. The time had come to seek spirits elsewhere.

A Wedding Feast

I HAD MY DINNER of lambchop, peas, potatoes and orange tomato at a pub down the street from the Cashel Hotel, where I was staying. A cozy, shabby pub. When I first entered the pub there were only two other customers. An old thin gent in his tattered gray coat, dirty trousers and shoes, faded tweed cap and a two days' growth of beard and a look-alike friend. I ordered a pint, studied the menu and ordered my dinner at a cost of L.2.50. I took a seat at a table and waited a half-hour for my meal. Shortly after my meal was delivered to me by the very pretty, dark-haired, young barmaid, a wedding party arrived. The party consisted of the bride and groom, two other women around forty and a decrepit looking gentleman, probably the bestman. All were beyond the point of sobriety, but the groom was belligerently intoxicated.

It took me awhile to believe it was truly a wedding party and not just a group of characters sadly in masquerade. As the bride, the two women and best man sat down shoulder to shoulder, all cozy at a table, the groom went and stood at the bar, babbling on incoherently to the already stationed other two customers. At that point, since I was quite interested in my food, I wasn't taking much notice of these people aside from the dress of the bride and her bridesmaids. It looked a bit sad for them to be wearing their long, pink, frilly dresses amongst the comparative squalor. The groom's attire consisted of a black leather jacket and black trousers, white shirt and black necktie. The bestman wore a tattered sports jacket and an open-collared, frayed white shirt.

After the groom had stood for awhile mumbling to the customers at the bar, and the best man pulled a paper-wrapped sandwiched from his jacket pocket in preparation of dinner, the bride called out "Willie!" to her new spouse. There was silence and she repeated her request for a response: "Willie!", an elongated whiny cry so it took several seconds to pronounce.

(Ignored by Willie.)

"Willie!"

(More of the same from Willie.)

"Willie! Willllliiieee!"

Willie mumbled something to himself.

"Willllliiieee!"

"Aw, what the fuck d'ya want?" Willie finally replied.

"C'mon over and sit with your wife." "Aw, get off it! Can't ya see I'm talkin'!?"

The bride and her groom were about thirty, but seemed older because of the very haggard style of their ways.

When Willie refused to come sit with his bride, the bridesmaid remarked, "Oh, don't mind him, honey. He's just nervous, ya know."

"Willllliiieee!"

"Oh, fuck off!"

"Willie, come on now, love, sit with your wife."

"Come on now, Willie," said the bridesmaid, "Come over and sit with us."

"Aw, fuck it!" Willie moaned as he stumbled over to the reception table.

Willie sat down next to his wife, his head towards the floor, his hands clasped together between his knees, as a stream of smoke from his cigarette dangling from his lips caressed his eyebrows.

"Aw, come on now, Willie, give your wife some lovin," the bride said, pulling his right arm around her shoulder giving her wedding dress the benefit of a drop of cigarette ash. Willie apathetically allowed the gesture and the bridesmaid said, "Now, ya got him, Rita." Willie defiantly removed the confines of Rita and declared, "Aw, fuck off! Who's got me now? What's all this fuckin' business!?"

Rita sighed, "Now, come on, Willie, I'm your wife now. That means you're my husband. Like it or not, you're mine now!"

"Aw, fuck it!" Willie said and got up from his seat with the party and entered the back room, the pool table room.

"Now, don't worry, love, he's just nervous," the bridesmaid told Rita.

Soon the dark-haired pretty barmaid delivered several plates of Irish stew to the party's table. It was the official wedding feast. The party went on drinking, smoking and eating simultaneously. Rita called persistently for Willie. Willie refused to respond. "Aw, it's all right. He's just nervous."

The bestman asked the barmaid, "Where's Willie?" to which she turned and asked a young man who had just returned from the gents toilet. "He's all right, he's got a little chair for himself up there next to the pool table."

"Williiieee, come eat your dinner," Rita called into the back room.

"Aw, fuck it! I don't want no slop!"

"Leave him alone, Rita," the bridesmaid said. "He's just nervous." The rest of the party went on with the feast and Willie grew tired of no one calling for him. Stumbling down the steps from the pool table room to join the others he sat next to Rita, took one of the plates of food and placed his face inches from it as he shoveled in a few forksful of meat, potatoes and peas.

"Aw, this is fuckin' slop. I don't want no fuckin' slop."

"Oh, come on now, Willie, it's our weddin' night," Rita begged. "We're supposed to be having a good time."

"Aw, fuck it! What the fuck am I doing here!? You call this a wedding? I call it a fucking set up!"

I finished my meal, paid my bill and returned to the Cashel Hotel. I ordered a pint of Guinness and a measure of Bushmills at the bar and had just begun to sip my Guinness when Willie and Rita came stumbling into the room. Rita was still not as bad off as Willie, who was the picture of absolute drunkenness but she had done her best to catch up with him. Willie pushed his way between two seated customers and announced, "Hey, give us a pint o' Guinness here." The barmaid ignored him and he repeated his request. He was then told by the barmaid, "I'm sorry, sir, we can't serve you."

"Why not?"

"Because the bar is only for residents of the hotel."

"Aw, fuck it! Give me a pint."

"I'm sorry, I can't serve you."

Willie turned to the people through whom he had pushed and said with a drool, "What's she on about? I want a fuckin' pint and I'll bust up the place. That's right, I'll bust up this fuckin' place if I don't get me a fuckin' pint."

At that last remark, the barmaid called to the bouncer at the front door, who came over saying, "All right now, let's not have any trouble here. Just move along now."

"I'm not givin' ya any trouble and I'm not movin' along. I just want my fuckin' pint. Just ask my wife here. It's our fuckin' weddin' night and we want some fuckin' pints!"

Rita stood in the background. "Jesus Christ, Willie, don't disgrace yourself."

"Aw, fuck off! I just want a fuckin' pint."

"Come on, out with you and don't be any more trouble," the bouncer demanded.

"Aw, let's get outta here," Willie said to his wife, who now had her man.

"Jesus Christ, don't ever bring me back to this fuckin' town, Willie," Rita shouted.

I watched as the bouncer made sure that the bride and groom made their exit from the bar and they were heard as they went into the night, "I want me fuckin' pint!", and "Jesus Christ, don't ever bring me back to this fuckin' place. Jesus Christ! Me weddin' night, indeed!"

"Aw, fuck off!"

Dublin

While in Cashel I had booked ahead for a room at Wellington House and at that time told Oliver, the sixty-ish gent, who apparently handled most of the business there now, that I'd planned to be in Dublin around 5 o'clock. That was before I realized that the only train getting into Dublin would arrive around 1 o'clock. Once the train pulled into Heuston Station, I took a taxi to Wellington House for the cost of L3. When I arrived at the door of Wellington House, a small hand-written sign in the window read "Please knock. Bell not working." Neither was anyone at the house working since after several taps on the window no one came for my entry.

I stood within the cast iron gate, guarding my bags. After about fifteen minutes, a gentleman from two doors down came out with his dog. "Are you all right?" the man asked. I was glad to have him speak and I walked over to explain my situation. He told me that Oliver was usually away until at least four o'clock on Sundays and that he had a key for Wellington House and gave me entrance to my home in Dublin. I went downstairs to where the keys hung, took the key for Room Number One and took my suitcases up to my room. I wrote a note to Oliver explaining that I had arrived in Dublin earlier in the day than planned and how I was fortunate enough to have been let in by a neighbor.

Quite content now, I began my first leisurely stroll of the local Dublin streets during this visit. Naturally, I walked past Ryan's, with its big wooden doors locked up for the holy hours. I spotted Aidan O'Keefe standing with another gent outside the Deer Park Lounge and walked towards him. He was not wearing his customary hat, but he was leaning on his customary cane. He didn't notice me until I was just steps away and it took a few seconds for him to recognize me. But shortly he smiled and I extended my hand and he shook it saying, "Good man! Taylor, is it?" Well, close enough, I figured. "Tyler," I gently corrected. He introduced me to his companion, Sean, and then Aidan and I walked across the street to the front of his bicycle shop, since one of his daughters was there. She was a very good-looking woman and I enjoyed having a short talk with her.

I told Aidan that I had appreciated receiving his St. Patrick's card this past year.

"I also received a Christmas card from Mr. Ryan."

Aidan leaned on his cane and I studied his heavily browed eyes as they misted and he said to me while I was still speaking, "There's been a bit of sadness since then." "I'm sorry for that. Do you want to tell me?" I wondered if he was going to tell me that Mr. Ryan had passed away.

I then knew what he was about to tell me. Aidan leaned more heavily on his cane, trembled, and a crack came to his voice as he said, "Nora...my wife...died. Last March."

I had known Nora briefly but well. She was a handsome woman and at least in appearance, several years younger than Aidan. It was apparent that she was good to and for Aidan. She was good to him in letting him make the rounds at the local bars and good for him by instilling a reminder to get home after closing time.

One evening Aidan made arrangements for Nora to share one of the two rear snugs at Ryan's with us. It was the only time I would see Nora in a bar and Aidan was delighted to hold court for the three of us while Mr. Ryan looked after our drinking needs. By the time of that evening I had known Aidan for a number of years and was flattered for Nora to tell me that Aidan spoke of me often and highly. In Aidan's presence I told Nora of my appreciation of his teaching me some words and expressions of the Irish language. How he watched me writing the first time I met him and said, "Ah, so it is citheog you are."

"What is that?" I asked him.

"Caggy-handed, you write with your left hand. Are you with me now, Taylor? Now, I want you to remember that; it's citheog you are and remember that it is your friend, Aido, that will teach you real Irish." "Yes," Nora happily recollected, "we spoke mostly Gaelic when we were young in Wexford before moving north to Dublin." She looked at Aidan with great affection and he beamed, "And what a wedding ceremony we had, Nora, the priest conducting the service in Irish and our vows shared in our native tongue. And I'll tell you something else; you are just as beautiful today as you were then, Nora." There had been some miles and several years between Dublin and the courtship in Wexford but the couple who had traveled them had not been distanced.

Aidan excused himself to visit the gents room and Nora spoke to me calmly, honestly. "You've known Aidan for some time now and I'm sure you are aware of how he can sometimes be forgetful. How he will often say the same thing over and over again, and how it may seem that it is just the drink that makes him unsteady on his feet. Or that age has dulled his mind. The fact of the matter is that as bright and friendly as he is, and no one knows better than I and our children that he is a wonderful man, he was once very brilliant. He was hit by a passing car, hitting his head on the pavement after closing time a few years ago and he hasn't been quite the same since."

When the doors of Ryan's close for the night, I was privileged to share with Nora the duty of helping Aidan cross the street. And the gentleman himself articulated his delight in being spoiled.

Sometimes Aidan would leave Ryan's before me for a drink or two at the Deer Park. But most of the time he would stay for the final pint with me and we would leave Ryan's crossing the street together minding the traffic light and taxi cabs. And sometimes the late night fog. A few times he insisted that I come in to share a nightcap of a cup of tea or a Powers. We always agreed upon the Powers. Once safely across the street we would approach his darkened bicycle repair shop, which housed dozens of bicycles and scattered parts. They were lined up against windows, hanging from bars on the ceiling, lying on wooden tables and on the floor. The tables, floors and walls smelled of decades' worth of lubricating oils and fluids.

"Hold my arm, Taylor, while I find my key," Aidan said as he steadied himself on his cane and reached into his tweed jacket pocket. "Now mind you, watch your step as I switch on the light. And don't make any noise or trip over anything." The silence of his shop was audible in contrast to the hours of voices at Ryan's. We came to the door leading to the living quarters and there was a scratching sound as the bottom of the wooden door scraped along the entry. Aidan repeated his admonition of silence as he lifted his right index finger to his lips. "Ssshhhhh!" he grinned and bounced his shoulders in silent laughter, then paused to listen if there was any sign of Nora hearing our entry. Confident that we had not awakened her he motioned for me to follow him. Just inside the doorway on the wall was a little plastic well under a portrait of Christ. Aidan whispered, "Here, dip your fingers in the holy water as you enter this house."

We walked quietly into the kitchen, which was straight ahead. "Now have a seat by the table and I'll fix us both a whiskey," Aidan said as he went to a cabinet above the refrigerator, took down a bottle of Powers and uncharacteristically turned his back to me. I admired the well lived-in kitchen. No true Irish kitchen is without a few unwashed teacups, saucers and butter knives scattered around and Aidan's kitchen was authentic in every way, speaking well of companionship. Aidan took a chair and joined me at the table with two glasses and handed me one containing translucent amber liquid. I thanked him; we raised our glasses in unison, made a toast to our friendship and putting the glass to my mouth sipped a dram of air. I looked over at Aidan and saw him very pleased with himself, having tricked me with a novelty shop gag glass, which had hollowed sides, which enclosed the fake drink. He grinned, then covered his mouth with his left hand since his right hand was holding a glass of real whiskey, and laughed, but not loudly as not to disturb Nora. "Now, Taylor, have you ever seen anything quite like this before?" I assured him that no, I hadn't and that I understood at that moment what he had been up to when his back was toward me. I had to admit that it was a good trick. He then took the glass from me, filled the real well with Powers and we continued with our after hours drink which extended to another before I carefully dodged bicycles and carts before walking back to Wellington House, very warm inside on a chilly November Dublin night.

From the first time I visited Dublin in 1976, I have always recalled the unique scent of the western part of the city. It is noticed mostly in the late hours of the afternoon as the sun is setting with the sky turning shades and streaks of red over the Four Courts and the winds blow towards O'Connell Street. It is heightened by the deep aroma of the Guinness Brewery and it could be considered Dublin's private perfume but it is much more robust. Perfume is much more likened to Paris, with its Seine and impressionistic, dainty pastels. Dublin's scent is as dark as the slow moving waters of the Liffey and as heavy and abrasive as the river's walls. It drifts along, not like a melodic song from an accordion, but like the drone of a cello and the lower register of a flute. It is as much a part of the character of Dublin as the Ha' Penny Bridge, Grafton Street, Trinity College, St. Stephen's Green, St. Patrick's Cathedral, street urchins or anything else the city is known for. The grandeur of the Shelbourne Hotel seems vaguely cloaked in artificiality when measured against the late afternoon air, as heady as single malt Irish whiskey.

Dublin's scent takes on an even more acute aspect in the fall when the groundskeepers of Phoenix Park are burning leaves and the smoke drifts out past the gate, down Conyngham Road and beyond Parkgate Street before it intermingles with the bus exhaust of Heuston Station and the chimney steam of the Guinness Brewery. After the autumn sun has set a mist settles. It is not a drizzle or a fog but a thick atmosphere that would not even be noticed if it were not illuminated by the street lamps and its quiet drama could only be enhanced if the burning of coal for residential heat were not now prohibited. In the west the scent of burning turf remains as it has for centuries but the night air of Dublin has lost something in the name of progress while retaining a character all its own.

Diversion

EACH NIGHT AT ten thirty Mr. Ryan flipped the light switch up and down three times, signaling last chance for customers to order drinks. It is not enough to say that it was a signal for last call. It was a beacon for a slight but noticeable frantic surge. Those having seats at the bar are the first to acquire consideration for another pint or another whiskey. Some of the ladies drink Irish coffee or wine. But mostly the pint glasses, empty, half-empty or full, have arms outstretched between the bartenders and customers, traded like dancing partners. Some of the customers order two drinks as their final request before of the execution of drinking time. These are the lucky ones, the people at the bar. The others in the crowded room who are standing three and four deep must make their way through backs, elbows and shoulders before getting as far as the back of an occupied bar stool. It is the DMZ of Ryan's and gaining such ground without stepping on someone or being stepped upon or being splashed by stout is a successful but never guaranteed maneuver.

"Excuse me" and "Pardon me" are more often than not wasted efforts to gain consideration by members of the crowd. It is a basic formality of shoving. Orders for pints are shouted over, under and between heads. It is the nightly ritual of cacophony. The bartenders pour pints, take orders, take money and make change flowingly. They automatically line up rows of pints; first filling them half full, then three-quarters full, allowing them to settle before the final topping of the muddy-colored head. One by one each is delivered to an eager customer who returns the favor by exchanging an empty glass of foamy residue. At ten-fifty Mr. Ryan began the nightly choir of "Time please, ladies and gents." The official time for finishing drinks was eleven p.m.

The unofficial time was eleven-thirty. At least in Ryan's. There are the clubs around O'Connell Street where the die-hard night-lifes can pay a few pounds for a few extra hours of drinking surrounded by impossibly loud music.

Many nights I would feel the increase of my drink as the lights dimmed at Ryan's. Aidan would be finishing the last of his pint and Powers and he needed guidance getting down the block and across the street to his bicycle shop and home. By ten past eleven Mr. Ryan would shout, "Now, time, please ladies and gentlemen! We are way past our time now! Time, please ladies and gents." As the room slowly emptied, one of the bartenders went through a trap door behind the bar next to the change box to the basement and brought up cases of supplies for the next day. Plenty of four ounce bottles of "lemonade," a soda for mixing with gin or vodka plus bottles of wine, whiskey and bottled Guinness for those who preferred it to kegged stout. Other bartenders would stack the chairs and sweep the cigar and cigarette butts from the floor.

Some people are naturally or defiantly impervious to signs of closing time. Aidan was of the former. He spoke to the older gents, those who had known Ryan's before its current celebrity. Aidan was a member of a small congregation that is no longer. Aidan and I were the last to leave more than once. One night it was our last time to leave together. He became uncomfortable with the influx of latter day patrons of Ryan's. "Sure this is a fine place and you spend a few extra coppers for a good pint. But there are other places for a drink just within walking distance and it's always good to go for some diversion. Are you with me there, Terry?" No need or reason to attempt a response as Aidan repeated and defined his case - "I know of some places within these blocks that serve just a' good a' pint as here. They may not be as fancy as here and God bless it. But you've got to get some diversion. You've got to see more. Are you with me? You've got to spend more time with diversion."

I told him that I would be glad to go for some diversion with him some other night. At the moment it was time to let the patient bartenders at Ryan's close for the night. The large wood doors closed behind us and the copper lock was set in place until opening time late the following morning.

Aidan held on to my right elbow as we walked slowly down Parkgate Street. Even with his cane, he needed extra support to walk steadily. It was more his age and the darkness than the drink. "Are you ready for another pint now?" he asked. "That would be fine but everything is closed now," I said. "Now, then," he argued, "haven't you paid attention to what I've told you about diversion? Come with me, and mind you now, just be quiet about it."

We walked several more yards and stopped at a darkened pub. It was clear by looking through the curtains that it was closed. The only light came from the red neon of the Guinness clock above the bar. Aidan took a quick look around and the nearby sidewalks were empty except for the two of us. He gently tapped his cane on the basement window. We waited a moment by the dark veiled curtain. He tapped again and in a few seconds a hand slowly folded the curtain back and a face appeared through the window. There was a gesture without words that said "Wait there" and in a few moments a shadowy figure, slightly outlined by the Guinness clock, came through the bar.

The front door opened and a gentleman said, "How are ye tonight, Aidan? Come on in and just be quiet about it." "Thank you, thank you," Aidan said as the door silently closed behind us. "I'd like you to meet my friend from America. New Jersey, New York." We were escorted through the dark to a landing of steps leading to a dimly lit bar downstairs. There were about six other gentlemen having afterhour diversions of pints and whiskies.

Aidan introduced me to his friends and ordered two pints of Guinness, for which he let me pay. He continued his lecture to me on the civics of diversion. "You see, if you come here on a regular basis you can have an extra pint or two after closing time. Are you with me now, Terry? Are you winning?" "Winning" was Aidan's expression for enjoying a drink. Occasionally he used "winning" to mean on the way to becoming intoxicated. I was winning with a half pint to go of my first taste of diversion. I lifted the glass towards my mouth when Aidan touched me on my shoulder and said, "Put your glass down." I continued to bring the glass to my mouth, figuring that whatever Aidan had to say could wait until after another sip. He repeated sternly, "Put your glass down now." As I did so I looked around the bar to see all other customers looking towards the stairway. The glasses sat abandoned on the bar. A pair of Garda came down the stairs, over to the bar, demonstrating their official presence.

"What's going on here at this hour?" one Garda demanded.

"We are just finishing our last round of tonight's drink," the proprietor said. It was an obvious lie. The Garda responded, "You know as well as I do that closing hour is way past. Is this a political meeting you're having here?"

"No. We're just having a few drinks and then we're closing."

"Is that right? You're sure this isn't a political meeting?" It was a formality of questioning. The customers, except for myself, were familiar faces.

"Well, we'll direct you all to leave now since it's well past closing time and we won't press any charges. Be on with you now."

I aided Aidan with his cane up the stairs towards the front door. "This bar is closed," one of the Garda said to the bartender. "But before you lock the doors, pour us both a pint." The officers sat down, removed their hats, placed them on the bar and waited patiently for their drinks.

One morning I flew to Dublin from London after staying with friends in Northampton and Guilford, England. Arriving at Dublin airport I was one of two passengers whose luggage did not pass through long strands of plastic flaps, on to the rotating carousel. We had come in on a British Air flight and when we asked the fate of our belongings we were told to go to a "Baggage Inquiry Desk" with just a small bit of hope that our bags would come in on the next British Air arrival from London due in about an hour. After filling out forms for lost luggage we waited for the next transference of baggage. The next British Air flight arrived on time with still no trace of our baggage.

We returned to the inquiry desk and had our baggage claim forms fed into a computer and were advised to have a seat and wait for a security representative to "get back to us." After another twenty minutes a security officer approached the woman and told her, without looking at me at all, "We have learned that your bag will be coming in with the one-forty-five flight from London. Our computer baggage check showed that your bag just ended up on a later Dublin flight. It happens infrequently but it happens nonetheless." The woman explained that she needed to catch a train to Killarney and would not be able to wait around until one-forty-five because of the train departure. She was assured that the airport would arrange for her baggage to be sent by rail to Killarney later that day.

The security guard then turned to me and said, "I'm afraid I've got no good news for you. The number on your baggage claim ticket does not show up on our computer. That means there is no indication of it being cleared for transport on any flights today."

"So that could mean that my suitcase could be anywhere in Europe now."

"That's one way of putting it and I'll agree it's a viable assessment. These things usually work out about 99% of the time but in this case I can't guarantee that your suitcase will show up." I didn't know quite how to react so I just thought to myself, "You're in Ireland now and there has got to be a glimmer of hope."

"There's no sense your waiting around here any longer. Do you have an address in Dublin where you can be reached?"

I filled out another form, indicating the address of Wellington House and took a city center bus from the airport to Heuston Station, which is just a short walk between Ryan's and Wellington House. I went directly to Ryan's for a pint and was cordially greeted by John Ryan and Mick, a bartender at the pub for forty-two years. "Well, it's back again with us, are you? How long are you here for?" John asked.

"It kind of depends on when and if I get my suitcase," I said in mentioning the experience at the airport.

"What airline were you on?"

"British Air."

"Well, it serves you right and I hope that teaches you something. If you had flown Aer Lingus none of that would have happened."

I had a second pint and looked past the large hanging globe lamps and out the window with the reversed letters of RYAN'S WINES AND SPIRITS and admired a sudden snow squall upon a swift wind. It was the perfect opportunity for a walk and as I made my way to Wellington House the snow turned to hail and bounced along the pavement like millions of tiny glass marbles and ended the moment I reached the iron gate.

After a reunion with Gerry, the proprietor of the house, my good friend and occasional drinking partner of many years, I went to my room, #1, just at the top of the red carpeted stairs, the walls lined with reproductions of paintings of the battle of Waterloo. I poured a whiskey, sat in the chair by the bed with my feet propped up, and drifted to sleep, gazing out the window at the leaden gray sky over Phoenix Park.

About an hour and a half later a strong tapping came on the door downstairs, rousing me from sleep. Unfolding my arms from my chest and removing my feet from the foot of the bed I got up convinced that the tapping could only mean one thing. Before I could get down the stairs, the tapping turned to pounding. Through the glass on the door I saw a taxi and its driver delivering my suitcase.

I thanked the man and asked him if I owed him anything.

"Oh, no, sir. It's all been taken care of by the airport."

Several stickers were pasted on the suitcase by British Air Security. "Hand inspect," "Date," "Removed after X-rays," and a hand written note, "Tripod. OK. Cleared for transport." My tripod had been mistaken for something suspicious, perhaps a pipe bomb during a conveyor belt x-ray check.

It was time to return to Ryan's and look up my friend Aidan to share pints and conversation and perhaps some diversion. I wouldn't be in a corner scribbling away letters and journal pages, but would celebrate an evening of paying attention to my friend. I walked a quick pace down Conyngham Road to No. 28 Parkgate Street, opened one of the large doors and entered the crowded pub. I was able to find an available seat and the sight of a bespeckled Mr. Ryan tending to business in his black trousers, white shirt and black vest. In a short time he spotted me and approached, shook my hand and smiled with his eyes over his eyeglasses, which rested on the lower bridge of his nose. There were other bartenders so it was a privilege to have this rare remainder of a dying breed: a courtly gentleman come to serve me in his own establishment. "Well, hello and welcome back. You look well so I suspect all is right in the world with you. Is it a Guinness I can get for you?"

"Yes, please, one of your fine pints, Mr.Ryan."

"Good man, good man."

Mr. Ryan poured the pint, let it settle for a few minutes, filled the glass again, let it settle one more time, topped it off and delivered it to me. "I trust all is right in the world with you," he said again placing the glass before me.

"All is well, but I must ask you something. I was here earlier today and thought I might find Aidan. There is no sight of him here now. Perhaps he is in another pub but he is generally here at this hour. Can you tell me how he is?"

Mr. Ryan extended a look of grimness, which turned into straightforward condolence.

"It is my sad duty to inform you that Aidan is beneath the clay. It was about a year ago. He was just never the same after Nora died. Wouldn't take any help from anyone when he crossed the street. So he was on his own after closing time and got hit again by a passing car. He lost consciousness and never came out of it."

"So then, to Aidan," as I had a silent ceremonial communion of the parting glass.

Glengariff Revisited

IN EARLY APRIL of 1992 I was informed of the death of a man who had been my best friend in fourth and fifth year of grammar school. Our main link at ages nine and ten was rivalry for the affection of the same girl in our class, who teased us equally insufferably. In the end we were both forsaken for an interloper. As did many in our high school class, my former best friend left town after graduation, never to return except for an occasional visit with his immediate family. I never saw him again. Word had it that he had suffered a heart attack at a friend's home during a dinner party and fell face first into his main course, dying on the spot, leaving a wife and two children.

I attended the funeral, which was held at the local church of his boyhood and after the ceremony went to the home of his mother. There was a traditional gathering of family and friends, food and drink. At this impromptu reunion I met the best friend from high school years of the girl, who had initiated the first fatal blow of unrequited love. Even casual contact had been severed after that. I asked of Patty and was told that her husband had died two years earlier, leaving her with two young girls. I asked that my condolences and best wishes be relayed and a few weeks later I received a letter which began several months of correspondence, shortening a distance of thirty years to two hundred miles.

For several years Ireland had been my private refuge, my new home, with Dublin in particular always attracting me with all of its honesty of grittiness composed in memory in black and white, much more so than the ascending colors of Dublin Castle or the Shelbourne Hotel. Ryan's Pub was, for a time, the meeting place and dividing line between the neighborhood working class regulars who had known generations at the pub and who now scorned the growing number of what they called the yuppies, the ones who were squandering a century of quiet tradition for crowded hot plate lunches.

Traveling alone provided the convenience of making my own destinations and time schedules. There was never lack of company in any city, town, village or hamlet, bus ride, train ride, boat ride, guest house or pub. A visit anywhere was guaranteed of conversation either welcomed or unsuccessfully avoided. Patty had never been to Ireland but began reading and developing a strong interest in the land, its people and centuries of culture. She urged me to take her along on my next visit and while I was reluctant for quite awhile, she was finally convincing.

The first week of October 1993 Patty was in Dublin with me. We spent the evenings in the pubs, most importantly Ryan's, the Palace Bar and the Brazenhead. We next headed west to Galway. I phoned a friend in Salthill, whom I'd first met in 1976. I always stayed at her guesthouse while in Galway. She always had a full pot of tea and freshly baked Galway pastries waiting by the turf fire in the non-smoking lounge. It was the beginning of Patty and me traveling the west of Ireland together.

We returned in May of 1995, going to Glengariff after several days in Galway and Kerry. Late in the afternoon we took the only route, the road from Kenmare. The ride is a harrowing experience at best. All high altitudes narrow bends, no barricades, a road just wide enough for single lane traffic although accommodating traffic in both directions, an excavated tunnel near the summit with no hint of what followed it. Every inch of the long stretch of potential tumbling off the mountain drive must be shared evenly and slowly. Backing up was never an option.

While Patty drove I sipped my flask of whiskey. It was a measure of the terror of the drive that with all of the panoramic views of the distances ahead and below we took no photographs. The journey lasted about an hour before the descent into Glengariff, where, happy to be on flat land we paused to take a few photographs of road signs and a deserted Mobil gas pump. I celebrated by drinking more whiskey while Patty celebrated by smoking cigarettes. After that it was easy traveling to the center of Glengariff. We parked in front of the Blue Pool Hotel where I had returned for a second visit ten years earlier. I approached the hotel. During the course of ten years the hotel, which had been the centerpiece of the village, where years of welcomes to friends and strangers, good talk, laughter, fine meals and service were known, was now a dark and empty shell. The unwashed windows to the dining room looked solemnly into the past. The large wooden cabinets and their contents of china and silver were gone. Tables and chairs, which had welcomed guests, were replaced by markings of legs of age.

Across the street the Spinning Wheel woolen shop was fully alive and in business. Sheepskins were still piled by the entrance as their ancestors had been years earlier. I went over to the shop hoping to find a familiar face. I recognized no one but noticed the shop had expanded to having an upstairs tearoom. A young man by the cash register asked if he could help me and I asked if he had any details of the closing of the Blue Pool.

"The owner died and soon after the place shut down."

"The owner, Paddy, you mean."

"Yes, Paddy. I take it then that you knew him?"

" Yes, I knew him. He owned half of Glengariff, you know."

"Yes, that's right, or at least that's what he liked to have us believe. Well, he died and he had a son who was supposed to take over the business."

"Had a son, you mean he died too?"

"No, no, not like that. It's like this. Paddy's son was to take the place over and even while Paddy was still alive, it had been running downhill. First the paintings went. Then the sets of silver in the drawing room. Then the best of the furniture. The outside hadn't been painted in years. Well, then, there's not much more I can tell you beyond that. It didn't take long after Paddy died that the place was sold under what is best described as mysterious circumstances. His son sold the hotel to a corporation. Even the chains are buying up the old places these days. It saves them the trouble of building. It could be Juries for all we know. The last anyone heard is that the hotel is supposed to be refurbished and back in business in a few years, but as you can see, nothing over there has improved any just yet. Well, no one around here knows any more details and the son's whereabouts are unknown, except to him, of course."

"And what about John, who used to tend the bar. Do you know him?"

"No, I've heard of him, but I've never met him. I never see him in the village but understand he is still living with his wife in their home down the road towards Bantree. He's ill of health, I hear."

I asked the young man if he could recommend a guesthouse in the village and he suggested the River View. Patty and I followed the path on a newly paved road, passed the vacant decaying home of the old gentleman who had fixed my boot years ago. The house was empty and locked with unbearded windows. The brides and grooms on faded newspaper clippings still inhabited the walls.

At the River View guesthouse Patty and I were greeted by a gentleman in his sixties, who showed us to our room. While comfortable, the house was without nostalgia. Patty and I then walked directly to the Blue Loo bar for some pints and talked to the barman and the other customers about the ride from Kenmare, asking of any other way to get to our next destination, Killarney.

"Oh, yes, that is quite a scenic ride from Kenmare. If the view scares you, next time do it at night."

We thanked our new friends and walked back into the village with a light buzz of alcohol under the soft sun, happy to be on foot. Dinner was lamb chops and pints and the Cottage Bar. Before returning to River View house we drove to the entrance of the steep, narrow road to Barley Lake. I wanted to return to the place where the wind had knocked me off the rock, severing the heel from my boot. We approached the steep, winding road, but turned back after a quarter mile. It would have been pure masochism to continue on that ride after our experience on the road from Kenmare. We drove back to the village passing the church, which was overflowing with white-robed children celebrating first communion. A quiet evening was settling in Glengariff.

The day's drive had taken its toll on Patty. "You stay, drink and reminisce," she told me at the Blue Loo after we had returned for some planned hours' worth of pints. I remained for two more pints but left early without stopping in any more pubs, since there was no music in Glengariff that night.

I left the Blue Loo, went down the street past the boot repairman's house with its darkened windows and empty interior and paused by the stream, which flowed from the Blue Pool. At night with the lights of the village in the distance the darkness mixed with the sound of the stream slowly flowing over the ancient rocks deceptively seemed to have Glengariff little changed over the past decade. I entered the front door of the guesthouse and went up the stairs past the table lamp illuminating the reception room and the dining room behind it. Patty was sleeping while I quietly entered our room. I kept the light out while getting ready for sleep. Outside the bedroom window a dim moonlight shone upon the garden of leprechauns. I heard John admonishing me and only half-smiling thought, they have moved closer to the village, out of the forest, leaving their bicycles and laundry behind, since the village has more need for them now. There was John, twelve years earlier, having lost his patience, telling me that in all of his forty years of tourism, he'd never heard of such talk of foolishness. The garden fixtures were not real leprechauns. The tales that Christine, Richard and I had told John were not real. But memories are real. In all of his forty years of tourism, I thought, looking into the garden, John must have seen many times that fantasy is the heart of real life and that it is much easier to believe than silent, empty, undusted rooms where there was once laughter and talk. Rooms, which waited for new tales, alive with fantasy of the little people, instead of a building where there are now only ghosts.

All Its Own

FROM THE FIRST time I visited Dublin in 1976, I have always recalled the unique scent of the western part of the city. It is noticed mostly in the late hours of the afternoon as the sun is setting with the sky turning shades and streaks of red over the Four Courts and the winds blow towards O'Connell Street. It is heightened by the deep aroma of the Guinness brewery and could be considered Dublin's private perfume but it is much more robust. Perfume is more likened to Paris, with its Seine and impressionistic, dainty pastels. Dublin's scent is as dark as the slow moving waters of the Liffey and as heavy as the abrasiveness of the river's walls. It drifts along, not like a melodic song from an accordion, but like the drone of a cello and the lower register of a flute. It is as much a part of the character of Dublin as the Ha'Penny Bridge, Grafton Street, Trinity college, St. Stephen's Green, St. Patrick's Cathedral, street urchins or anything else the city is know for. The grandeur of the Shelburne Hotel seems vaguely cloaked in artificiality when measured against the late afternoon air, as heady as single malt Irish whiskey.

Dublin's scent takes on an even more acute aspect in the fall when the groundskeepers of Phoenix Park are burning leaves and the smoke drifts out past the gate, down Conyngham Road and beyond Parkgate Street before it intermingles with the bus exhaust of Heuston Station and the chimney steam at the Guinness Brewery. After the autumn sun has set a mist settles. It is not a drizzle or a fog but a thick atmosphere that would not even be noticed if it were not illuminated by the street lamps and its quiet drama could only be enhanced if the burning of coal for residential heat were not now prohibited. In the west the scent of burning peat remains as it has for centuries but the night air of Dublin has lost something in the name of progress while retaining a character all its own.

It is best not to know when one is saying good-bye.

All of Dublin will continue to change. The permanence of scaffolding speaks of the city's constant alteration. All of Dublin will remain the same. The gray light of Dublin is eternal. Businessmen, students and tourists still crowd the bars at lunch time, after work, and on until closing time. Bewley's will serve coffee, tea, pastries, soups, and sandwiches for the hordes of Grafton Street. The lines gather each morning for the opening of Burdick's Fish and Chips.

But one little corner of Dublin has changed forever, altering my vision yet unintentionally keeping part of me there.

Ryan's has been sold. Wellington House has been sold. Jerry has moved to Kildare, raises horses and Aidan is with Nora. His bicycle shop still stands across the street from the newsagent on the corner of Parkgate Street. The paint is slowly fading from his shop but "Aidan O'Keefe" still looks out across Parkgate Street. There are still bicycle parts inside the shop, whose windows have thickened with darkness. There is a tiny trough of plastic where the holy water has long since evaporated.

I got into a taxi heading to the airport one morning by the gate of my residence on Conyngham Road and while passing Ryan's asked the driver if he ever stopped for a pint there. "Oh, no, I'm off the drink. Have been for years but I know of the place well. It's become very popular these past few years."

"Yes, I know."

The sun was rising over the Grand Canal, burning its way through the clouds over the Ha' Penny Bridge, and illuminating the steam which hung horizontally over St. James Gate. The flat bed trucks with their Guinness barrels rumbled from the brewery for their hundreds of city destinations. The newsagent and the shop serving breakfast were the only establishments open on Parkgate Street. Outside the betting office swirls of racing forms waited for the daily customers to return for better luck. Dogs rummaged through overturned garbage pails. In Phoenix Park the groundskeepers were beginning their work day by digging up huge beds of geraniums before the first frost, tossing them into pickup trucks. Other workers raked leaves into piles to be burned into a smoky smolder later in the day. I would leave Dublin before the first match was taken to the leaves. Lazily and lightly the scent of autumn leaves would hover over the park and then with a breeze flow down the path where Conyngham Road and Parkgate Street meet. A sudden eastern wind would carry the smoke in the opposite direction towards the iron gate, which had closed behind me for the last time. If I ever return to that corner of Dublin in autumn, the burning leaves will be a constant reminder of what has faded away. And being painfully playful, not allowing me to completely let go of what once was.